A GUIDE TO

LONDON

readcereal.com

CEREAL

CITY GUIDES

———

SAY HELLO

hello@readcereal.com

BE A STOCKIST

stockist@readcereal.com

ROSA PARK

Editor

RICH STAPLETON

Creative Director

———

———

RICHARD ASLAN

Sub Editor

JON RICH

Illustrator

Photography by **Adrienne Pitts, Rich Stapleton, Ash James** & **Toby Mitchell**

Words by **Richard Aslan, Rosa Park, Ruth Ainsworth** & **Robbie Lawrence**

Published by Cereal Ltd.

Printed in the United Kingdom on FSC certified uncoated paper.

THE CONCEPT

We at *Cereal magazine* have travelled to cities around the world and sought out places that we believe to be unique, interesting, and enjoyable. Our aim is to produce guides that would befit *Cereal* readers and modern travellers alike, recommending a tightly edited selection of experiences that combine quality with meticulous design. If the food is top notch, so too is the space that accompanies it. You'll soon notice that our version of the perfect trip is woven in with an understated flair and a penchant for grand landscapes – both natural and manmade.

These guides complement what we do at *Cereal magazine*. Our print title is focussed on the timeless, the cultural, and the historical. We often discuss the language, local cuisine, architecture, and classic sights of a destination, so our city guides are its welcome counterpart. Here you'll find the practical advice you need on where to stay, where to eat, what to see, and where to shop. Together, the magazine and city guides form a holistic approach to travel that we live by.

THE GUIDE

This guide to London features a considered selection of shops, hotels, restaurants, cafes and points of interest. Not intended to be comprehensive, we present a discerning edit of our favourite places to visit in the city.

All photographs and copy are original and exclusive to Cereal.

TABLE OF CONTENTS

UNITED KINGDOM   ✈ LHR / GAT   💬 ENGLISH   ¤ GBP   📞 +44

LONDON

*I*n most great capitals, the statues tell stories of régime-change, revolution and upheaval. The marble and bronze denizens of London, however, have never been beheaded, unseated or evicted to an out-of-town retirement zone. The story of this city is one of relentless continuity. While it can no longer be counted among the world's largest metropolises, it remains redolent of Empire and the soot-laden might of the Industrial Revolution. Unrivalled in finance and at the forefront of fashion, tourists throng its streets. A truly global city, its residents not only speak over 300 languages, they also walk with an undeniable swagger.

ESSAYS: *My London*

James Lohan

Co-founder | MR & MRS SMITH

T here is so much to this city – so many lives being lived, and so many stories unfolding – that it is easy to feel lost in the clamour and throb. There are, however, unexpected pockets of serenity. As much as I love the pace of London, with its astonishing restaurant scene, and the cultural rollercoaster of pop up events and exhibitions, I'm not sure I could handle it without the counterpoised calm of the riverbanks and abundant greenery. We spent a good few years living on a houseboat in Chiswick, and I thrived on the contrast between the frenetic energy of running a business by day, and the tranquil roll of the Thames by night. The arrival of our children forced us back onto dry land, and now, whenever we need to wind down, we head to calming spaces such as Chiswick House and Gardens. This neo Palladian villa – handily, just a few moments from our home – is attractive in itself, but it is the gardens that wow me the most. Sitting in the cool, contemporary cafe, looking out over the grounds, is probably about as relaxed as I get.

When you have lived in London for a while, it becomes easy to overlook things. You become increasingly baffled at the tourists flocking to certain places, when there are other, far more interesting sights they could be seeing. On lazy weekend mornings, for example, we often head to Alfie's Antique Market in Marylebone, and just meander through the treasures there. You won't find that in most guidebooks. It is too easy to become jaded, losing the outsider's eye for what makes London so special to the millions who come here to experience it. That's why I count myself lucky to run a business within the travel industry. I am compelled to keep track of the comings and goings of the ever evolving hotel scene, and I am constantly reminded of what the appeal of my city is to visitors. I love seeing it with fresh eyes.

You would think that there simply would not be enough space in Piccadilly for it, but Kit Kemp's bold and quirky new Ham Yard Hotel nevertheless manages to cram in a theatre space and a bowling alley alongside the bedrooms. In-the-know eyes have also been fixed on – and fixated with – André Balazs's Chiltern Firehouse in Marylebone. It seems that no celebrity column is complete without a mention of whichever international A-lister was last seen spilling into the night from Nuno Mendes's incredible restaurant. The food may be fabulous, the décor perfectly judged, and the staff drilled to flawlessness, but for me, the big draw is the bar (residents only after 9pm). It is essentially a film star's lounge, with vinyl turntables as a centrepiece, and a sunken bar to which you can pull up an armchair and watch the bartender mixing miracles. Sitting up at the bar is one of the great joys of this city. It places you in prime people watching position to catch the to and fro of London life, gives you an inside view of how the business flows, and brings you into chance contact with a whole host of characters and ideas. It is handy for getting a quick drink too. Given the choice between dining at a table, or dining up at the bar, I will often plump for the latter. It somehow feels closer to the heart of things.

Summing up London is no easy task, but for me, it is the perfect balance of familiar and frenetic. It is a place that is packed with unique details, serendipitous finds, and the most incredible history – a history that is both personal and to be shared. It is where we started our first business, where we got married, and where we had a family. For those reasons, it will always be home.

Alex Eagle

Creative Director | ALEX EAGLE STUDIO

I'm a born and raised Londoner — I've never lived anywhere else. London to me is so many things, and so broad. It's my upbringing in leafy West London, in a big house with a garden for my brother and I to play, where the milk still came to the door in curvy glass bottles. It's my teenage years in Knightsbridge, where I went to high school and walked down Sloane Street every day, ogling the latest collections in the windows with my girlfriends. It's my twenties in Notting Hill, nodding good mornings to the local shopkeepers on Portobello Road and sipping cocktails in cosy, hidden bars. And now it's a loft in Soho, a place full of characters, humming with the urban buzz.

Sloane Street is really where I fell in love with fashion and design. When I was at school, it was such a hub and incredibly stylish, and all the stores — Joseph, Equipment, Gucci, Dolce & Gabanna — were there. Later, I lived on Walton Street in Chelsea, and opened my first store at 91 Walton, across the road. It was basically a shopable townhouse and an extension of my apartment, representative of where I was at that stage in my life. We outgrew that lovely space, and moved to Soho in April. It's funny how the new studio mirrors my Soho loft. I think your home is always a reflection of your life. Living in Soho means I can walk everywhere, from Regent's Park to Mayfair. It's an incredible blend of heritage and innovation: new boutiques, cafes and restaurants are always popping up, so there's a smorgasbord of experiences to try. Despite being in central London, it still feels, like many parts of London do, like a village. There's a real sense of community here.

I love showing people around London, and I think my ideal London day would be on foot. It's the best way to see everything, and it's such a walkable city. If I were planning the perfect walk for visitors, it would be through Soho and Covent Garden and down to The Strand to see The Courtauld Institute of Art and Somerset House. We'd then walk towards Embankment for the view from 180 The Strand next door. After that, I'd take them across the Embankment and along the river via the Tate Modern and onto The Globe Theatre, which is such a cross section of the modern and historic. Then, back over to St Paul's, which is just beautiful, before hopping in a cab to go to Knightsbridge for a drink — there's a lovely pub there called The Nags Head — and onto Pimlico to dine at La Poule au Pot.

London is full of hidden gems. There's a seemingly endless array of special places tucked away and lots of 'best kept secrets'. I love Society Club in Soho, for its beautiful books and cocktails — you can drink cocktails while you shop for books, which is pretty special. Petersham Nursery near Richmond is divine, like a little retreat from London. There's a cafe tucked inside the V&A Gallery courtyard, a hidden one in The Royal Academy and a beautiful one in the Wallace Collection. It's sort of a two for one: you go and soak up all that culture, then can sit down for afternoon tea and a treat. There's a hidden swimming pool under the Cafe Royal, and a spa nestled in the top floor of Fortnum and Mason. It's heavenly — like being in The Cotswolds while you're in the middle of London. There are many great museums to explore too. Charles Dickens House is wonderful, and the John Soane Museum is a real feast for the eyes.

London is extremely global, and I think that's reflected in the city's style and design. We have a strong English heritage that we hold onto, but we've now got great international influence too. It's a melting pot in every way. Having grown up here, my London is quite diverse and all-encompassing. To me, it's the best city in the world and it's my home. I've had many different lives within London in its different areas. There have been boyfriends and friends throughout the years in various parts of the city, which I've had a chance to explore. London is a bit of a juxtaposition: it's a green and peaceful city if you know where to find the secret oases, but it's also vibrant, urban and busy. The exciting thing about living here is that it can be both, and you figure out how to make London work for you — you learn where to get solitude and you know where to go to get inspired.

alexeagle.co.uk

PLACES TO GO

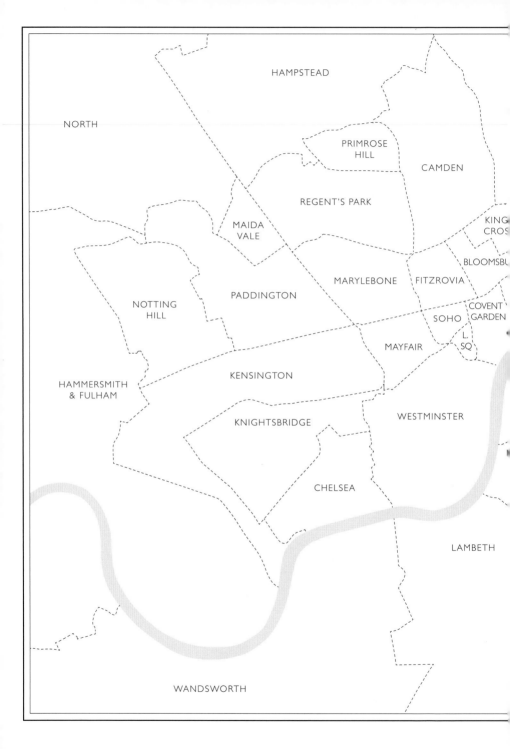

MAP OF LONDON

NGTON

HACKNEY

EAST

SHORE-
DITCH

ERKENWELL

BETHNAL
GREEN

N

CITY OF
LONDON

EAST END

H BANK

ON

GREENWICH

SOUTHWARK - LEWISHAM

○ NEIGHBOURHOODS

LONDON EDITION
Hotel

L ocated just off Oxford Street, in Fitzrovia, the London EDITION is a mix of classic baroque and modern lifestyle. A beautifully restored stucco ceiling furnishes the heights of the entrance lobby, and a large mirrored egg hanging from its centre highlights the contrast between contemporary design and the hotel's historic structure. The rooms are light and airy, and the wooden wall panels and oak flooring give a feel of an updated city townhouse. Each space features simple yet carefully considered accents, including mid century furniture and framed Hendrik Kerstens photographs.

📍 10 Berners Street, W1T 3NP

⭕ Fitzrovia

📞 020 7781 0000

➦ edition-hotels.marriott.com/london

BOUNDARY
Hotel

All 12 spacious guestrooms at The Boundary are staunchly modern in design, each one taking a cue from a renowned designer or design movement. The inspiration ranges from Le Corbusier and Mies Van Der Rohe to Scandinavian and Bauhaus. The five suites also come in distinct styles, with the added benefit of balconies and expansive views of the city. Spread over seven floors in a former printing factory, Terence and Vicki Conran's bespoke property has three restaurants – a French fine dining establishment, a rooftop bar and grill, and a café-bakery – keeping you well-fed and plied with drinks no matter the time of day.

📍 2-4 Boundary Street, E2 7DD

◯ Shoreditch

📞 020 7729 1051

➤ theboundary.co.uk

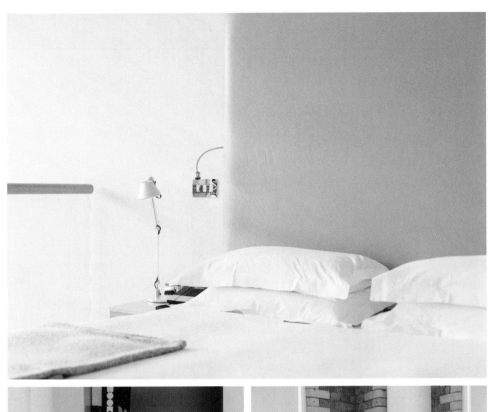

CHILTERN FIREHOUSE

Hotel

Chiltern Firehouse captures all the energy of Chiltern Street's lively stores and cafes with inimitable style. Andre Balazs knows how to do hospitality better than most, and the hotel offers the most exceptional and attentive service. A welcome drink and personalised stationery in the room are just a couple of the uplifting flourishes guests can expect. The bar, with its warm and lively interior, is a wonderful place to spend hours drinking, unwinding and people watching.

📍 1 Chiltern Street, W1U 7PA

◯ Marylebone

📞 020 7073 7690

↪ chilternfirehouse.com

LYLE'S

Restaurant

L yle's is all about the magic of juxtaposition. By taking two or three perfectly thought out elements and arranging them with skill and style, it all adds up to so much more than the sum of its parts. Evidence of this celebration of simplicity is found on the menu, with fresh honest dishes like anchovies, tomatoes and toast, or mackerel and gooseberries. It is also found in the décor, a three-part masterpiece comprising whitewashed walls, honeyed wood, and gallons of unfiltered daylight. Find them on the ground floor of the iconic Tea Building in Shoreditch.

📍 Tea Building, 56 Shoreditch High Street, E1 6JJ

◯ Shoreditch

📞 020 3011 5911

➤ lyleslondon.com

BAO

Restaurant

Bao, of course, serves exactly that – soft, pillowy steamed buns filled with a variety of big, addictive flavours ranging from fried chicken smothered in Sichuan mayo and *kimchi*, to confit pork layered with peanut powder. But the tantalising menu, based on Taiwanese street food, places equal emphasis on *xiao chi* (small bites). Our favourites from this section are mushrooms sprinkled with fragments of century egg and rectangular pig-blood cakes. The homemade peanut milk has a nostalgic, malty taste that makes for an ideal companion to your lunchtime meal. Though the queue for a seat is often long, Bao is worth the wait.

📍 53 Lexington Street, W1F 9AS

⭕ Soho

📞 N/A

➦ baolondon.com

THE CLOVE CLUB
Restaurant

A champion of seasonal, modern British cuisine, The Clove Club is the celebrated east London outpost of chef Isaac McHale. Here, a deliberately avant-garde set menu is served in a main dining room that manages to be both grand and spartan. With a cult following since launch, the restaurant also has a bar where guests can drop by for a drink and order snacks a la carte.

📍 Shoreditch Town Hall, 380 Old Street, EC1V 9LT

⭕ Shoreditch

📞 020 7729 6496

➡ thecloveclub.com

TYPING ROOM

Restaurant

Typing Room, headed by chef Lee Westcott and backed by Jason Atherton, offers contemporary fine dining in a casual, atmospheric setting. The tasting menu reads with deceptive simplicity, reflecting the intention to place natural ingredients and flavours centre stage. The food itself is presented with a certain theatrical decadence, yet executed with a skillfully light touch.

Patriot Square, E2 9NF

East End

020 7871 0461

typingroom.com

ST. JOHN BREAD AND WINE
Restaurant

S t. John Bread and Wine rests pristine amidst the crowds and noise of Spitalfields. As part of a group of restaurants that have only grown in reputation over the last two decades, this is an ideal place for a long, leisurely meal. Championing a rigorous devotion to simple, wholesome flavour, St. John plates up an ever evolving seasonal menu.

94-96 Commercial Street, E1 6LZ

Shoreditch

020 7251 0848

stjohngroup.uk.com

KOYA BAR

Restaurant

Koya Bar is a world dedicated to everything udon. This simple Japanese eatery in the heart of Soho strives to be honest, serious, and comfortable. It uses only the best ingredients to make sauces to dip, smother, and soak your noodles in. With a relaxed, sparse interior and food that tastes as good as it looks, Koya lives by the maxim 麺は地球 救う – "Noodle saves planet"

50 Frith Street, W1D 4SG

Soho

N/A

koyabar.co.uk

PORTLAND

Restaurant

The collective experience of the team behind Portland includes time spent at Quality Chop House, 10 Greek Street and Michelin-starred In de Wulf in Belgium, and this pedigreed group has come together to serve a bold, concise menu in a pared down setting. The best way to experience their food is to get a bit of everything and share amongst the table. Most memorable were the warm pumpkin cakes with chestnut, truffle and aged Mimolett, and the deer with salt baked celeriac.

📍 113 Great Portland Street, W1W 6QQ

⭕ Fitzrovia

📞 020 7436 3261

➤ portlandrestaurant.co.uk

MELROSE AND MORGAN

Deli and cafe

L ocated in Primrose Hill and Hampstead Village – two of London's greenest corners – there is something decidedly wholesome about Melrose and Morgan. This old style grocery shop and kitchen sells handmade and freshly prepared food to locals and visitors alike, and positions itself at the centre of a web of local fishmongers, butchers, and bakers to source most of its ingredients. From summer picnics to warming winter specials, this modern take on a traditional high street deli brings together the best from every season.

📍 42 Gloucester Avenue, NW1 8JD

⭘ Primrose Hill

📞 020 7722 0011

↱ melroseandmorgan.com

WORKSHOP COFFEE
Cafe

Established in 2009 by James Dickson, Workshop Coffee specialises in the sourcing and roasting of speciality coffee. Supported by an experienced roasting department, Workshop offers fresh and enthusiastically researched brews in its four locations around London, which includes its original Clerkenwell-based cafe and three coffee bars in Fitzrovia, Marylebone and Holborn. The company also hosts workshops on coffee making and its in-house dispensary distributes Workshop products around the UK. On a leisurely day, spend a quiet hour with a newspaper and a speciality blend in the back lounge of the Fitzrovia coffee bar, our favourite location.

📍 80A Mortimer Street, W1W 7FE

⭕ Fitzrovia

📞 N/A

↗ workshopcoffee.com

LISSON GALLERY
Gallery

Marina Abramović, Ai Weiwei, Gerard Byrne, Liu Xiaodong, Tatsuo Miyajima, Anish Kapoor; over four sleek storeys in dove grey and floor to ceiling glass, Lisson Gallery champions the game changers of contemporary art. Its forward looking collections are just as committed to showcasing the work of emerging talent. This is one of the longest established and most influential galleries in the world, and boasts spaces in NYC, Milan, and Singapore as well as London.

27 & 52 Bell Street, NW1 5DA

Marylebone

020 7724 2739

lissongallery.com

SERPENTINE GALLERY
Gallery

Hidden among the oaks and silver birches of Kensington Gardens sits the Serpentine Gallery. Formerly a 1930s tea pavilion, this red and grey brick edifice houses contemporary art exhibitions, displaying a diverse selection of subject matter including a permanent outdoor piece by artist and poet Ian Hamilton Finlay.

📍 Kensington Gardens, W2 3XA

◯ Kensington

📞 020 7402 6075

➤ serpentinegalleries.org

MARGARET HOWELL
Lifestyle store

The Margaret Howell store in Marylebone has the air of a downtown Tokyo art gallery. While the furniture, lighting, textiles, and clothing all exude a noticeably British aesthetic, there is a tangible sense of Japan in its clean oak panelled layout. Find hand woven Harris Tweed jackets and Mackintosh raincoats, alongside Anglepoise lamps and Robert Welch stainless steel cutlery.

34 Wigmore Street, W1U 2RS

Marylebone

020 7009 9009

margarethowell.co.uk

ALEX EAGLE STUDIO
Concept store

The imposing facade of this cool, eclectic concept store in Soho gives way to a fluid and personal retail space. Alex Eagle has a great eye and chooses only the best womenswear and lifestyle brands to place alongside her eponymous label, which blends a soft, classic elegance with inspired tailoring. Elsewhere in the store is an array of ceramics, art, accessories, and beauty ranges.

📍 6-10 Lexington Street, W1F 0LB

◯ Soho

📞 020 7589 0588

↪ alexeagle.co.uk

Folk

Menswear shop

Positioned just off of Brewer Street in the heart of Soho, this branch of Folk provides a selection of lighting and furniture pieces alongside their menswear edit in a bright, minimal space. Filled with an array of wardrobe staples like crewneck jumpers, shirting in varied fabrics and patterns, and classic outerwear from the British label's modern designs, this is the place to go for understated everyday clothing.

📍 24 Great Windmill Street, W1D 7LG

⭕ Soho

📞 020 7734 9466

➤ folkclothing.com

ANOTHER COUNTRY
Furniture & homewares shop

Located on Crawford Street, just outside the vibrant heart of Marylebone, Another Country's quieter location and subtle exterior are intentional. This interior and lifestyle destination is all about making furniture in the best way possible. Its collections are inspired by Shaker, Scandinavian, and Japanese style. They come complimented by a beautifully curated selection of homewares, linens, and handmade stationery from designers such as Carl Aubock and David Mellor.

18 Crawford Street, WH1 1BT

Marylebone

020 7486 3251

anothercountry.com

PERFUMER H

Fragrance shop

In the intimate, jewel-toned atelier of Perfumer H (designed by Retrouvius), hand-blown coloured glass fragrance bottles line the shelves and take centre stage. This retail concept comprises a working laboratory and shop, and is where perfumer Lyn Harris creates her scents. There are three categories of what's available: The Seasonal Editions range, which are scents that cover the five essential fragrance families of citrus, floral, wood, fern and oriental; The Laboratory Editions range, which further explores specific notes like rose; and home fragrance candles. And for something truly unique, there's the bespoke service: a private consultation where Harris makes a custom perfume just for you.

106A Crawford Street, W1H 2HZ

Marylebone

020 7258 7859

perfumerh.com

MOMOSAN

Homewares store

This Japanese homewares shop has its own charming brand of Zen, imbued with warmth and comfort. The gradually evolving edit of home accessories, ceramics, jewellery, teas, candles and other natural products never fails to introduce new and irresistible additions for the home. Owner Momo has a special flair for sourcing items you never realised you needed.

79A Wilton Way, E8 1BS

Hackney

020 7249 4989

momosanshop.com

MOUKI MOU
Lifestyle store

Behind Mouki Mou's simple white shop front on Chiltern Street is a clean and condensed collection of women's fashion and accessories. Rarer brands meet owner Maria Lemos' demand for careful craftsmanship and longevity, and visitors are encouraged to slow their pace and enjoy the experience. Discover beautiful new jewellery brands here, and get a good dose of active natural beauty products, with ranges such as Rodin and Susanne Kaufmann.

📍 29 Chiltern Street, W1U 7PL

⭕ Marylebone

📞 020 7224 4010

↪ moukimou.com

TRUNK LABS
Men's accessories shop

P acked with impeccable accessories, this small but stylish shop is the latest offering from Trunk Clothiers, a fixture on the Marylebone menswear scene since 2010. Trunk LABS has everything for the discerning gentleman to add a special something to his daily attire – luggage, bags, shoes, grooming products, eyewear – and there are even a few carefully chosen items of furniture to complement the look.

📍 34 Chiltern Street, W1U 7QH

⭕ Marylebone

📞 020 7486 2357

↪ trunkclothiers.com

DAUNT BOOKS
Bookshop

For over a century, Daunt Books has been selling an impressive collection of guides, phrase books, travel writing, history, and fiction from countries all over the world. The Marylebone High Street store is appropriately housed in an old Edwardian bookshop with long oak lined galleries, viridian walls, and expansive skylights creating a bright and cheerful interior.

83-84 Marylebone High Street, W1U 4QW

Marylebone

020 7224 2295

dauntbooks.co.uk

RIBA BOOKSHOP

Bookshop

Housed in RIBA itself, the RIBA Bookshop contains an exhaustive selection of architecture books, with plenty of shelves dedicated to design. Beautiful hardbacks and coffee table books abound; the sea of titles offers seemingly endless avenues of insight and investigation to explore.

66 Portland Place, W1B 1AD

Marylebone

020 7307 3753

ribabookshops.com

ADDITIONAL RECOMMENDATIONS

ACE HOTEL | *Hotel*

CHINESE LAUNDRY | *Restaurant*

HONEY & CO | *Restaurant*

J. GLINERT | *Shop*

KAFFEINE COFFEE | *Cafe*

THE LASLETT | *Hotel*

MONMOUTH COFFEE | *Cafe*

MONOCLE CAFE | *Cafe*

NATIONAL PORTRAIT GALLERY | *Gallery*

NATIVE & CO | *Shop*

NOPI | *Restaurant*

THE SCHOOL OF LIFE | *Shop*

TATE MODERN | *Museum*

TOKYO BIKE | *Bike shop*

TOWN HALL HOTEL & APARTMENTS | *Hotel*

CEREAL

CITY GUIDES

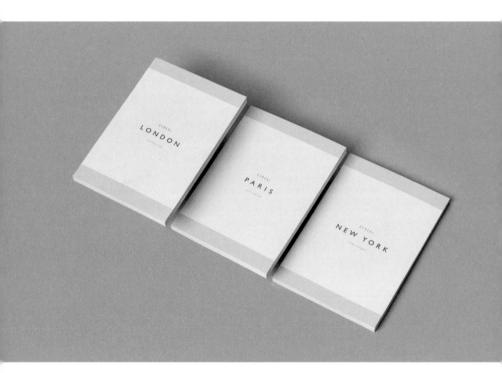

LONDON | PARIS | NEW YORK | COPENHAGEN

AVAILABLE AT

shop.readcereal.com